Echoes of You

A Collection of Love and Loss

NISHAN TANWEER

Copyright Page

Echoes of You: A Collection of Love and Loss

By Nishan Tanweer

Published by [Self Published]

ISBN:

For inquiries, contact: [tanweernishan@gmail.com]

Printed in India

About the Author

So let me introduce myself with a poetry,

I was whole once—

grounded, steady,

until life took everything,

one loss at a time.

Now I stand stripped bare,

emptied from the inside out,

a shell too tired to break,

too stubborn to fall.

But I'm still here—

not out of hope,

just because I have to be.

a collection of random poetry in no order about,

LOVE

HEARTBREAK

LONGING

MEMORIES

LOSS

PAIN

UNFINISHED LOVE

It all began in a silent space,
Lost in shadows, time erased.
Alone I sat, in endless gloom,
Locked away in my own tomb.

You knocked, you called, you begged, you swayed,
Said I deserved love, that I'd be okay.
Your voice like dawn, so soft, so true,
Yet fear still whispered, "They'll leave you too."

I saw the fire in your eyes,
A love so pure, it felt divine.
You searched for me in every place,
A restless heart, a desperate chase.

You prayed for me with hands so tight,
Asked the heavens every night.
You swore you'd stay, you'd never fade,
Yet doubts still wrapped me like a blade.

I loved you too, but fear held fast,
That love, like others, wouldn't last.
But now I see, through tear-stained view,
The light was real— **the light was you.**

I believed in you, in your gentle eyes,
In every promise, in every sigh.
I cherished all you did for me,
A love so deep, wild, and free.

But childhood storms had closed my soul,
Left me silent, never whole.
Yet with you, for the first time,
I spoke in truths, I let light shine.

I trusted you, I let you in,
Saw my world within your skin.
I thought at last, I'd found my stay,
A love that wouldn't fade away.

Yet deep inside, I always knew,
That fate would pull me far from you.
Still, your words had made me blind,
Believing you'd be **forever mine.**

I still remember, love, how you came,
Waiting for me, whispering my name.
How your heart beat for my voice alone,
How I was the only place you called home.

You wept to God with hands held tight,
Begging for me in the quiet night.
And oh, the fire in your jealous eyes,
When others stood too close, too nigh.

But love, it wasn't just you who cared,
I too had moments when I stared.
Yet I was blind to fate's cruel way,
That destiny would steal you away.

We used to sit and watch the moon,
Bathed in silver, soft and smooth.
I'd tell you, love, you shined far more,
Yet you'd deny it, unsure.

But oh, if only you could see,
The way your light looked back at me.
Your eyes—my answers, deep and true,
A world where only love once grew.

And when you smiled, when you stared,
Magic danced between the air.
I felt it all, but words fell shy,
For I was never good at why.

I know, my love, I hurt you so,
Left words unspoken, let love not show.
Not once did I mean to make you cry,
Yet silence cut us, passing by.

Each time I hurt you, love, believe,
It hurt me more than you could see.
For in my heart, so vast, so deep,
Was love too great for words to keep.

It wasn't just you who prayed at night,
With tear-filled eyes in dim moonlight.
I too begged God with whispered plea,
Crying, praying—**make you mine for eternity.**

You walked in like a gentle breeze,

Whispered love with such sweet ease.

Held my heart, made me believe,

Only to turn, only to leave.

Now I wake to silent screams,

Lost in nightmares, shattered dreams.

Panic grips, my soul undone,

A war within that can't be won.

How cruel it is to plant a rose,

Let it bloom, then let it go.

To build a home in someone's chest,

Then leave it burned, leave it wrecked.

Yet still my heart beats for you,

Though torn, though broken through.

I cannot hate, though pain runs deep,

Love still lingers where wounds weep.

You will not know the tears I cried,

The hollow ache I hold inside.

But one day, love, you'll taste this pain,

And you will cry in bitter rain.

For love is not a fleeting game,

Not a spark, then lost in flame.

And when regret comes calling true,

I hope it whispers—I loved you.

I still remember those tender days,

When you'd wake in tears, lost in a haze.

Dreaming you had let me go,

While I just smiled—I'd never go.

I held you close, calmed your fears,

Promised to stay for endless years.

Through every storm, through darkest skies,

I swore to never say goodbye.

But now, the silence haunts my soul,

A love once whole, now just a hole.

You walked away, left me behind,

Not even asking if I'm fine.

Did you ever pause, did you ever see,

The love you meant, the loss in me?

For though you've gone, my heart still stays,

Loving you in endless ways.

Love, I miss you more than words can say,

A hollow soul, lost in the gray.

Without you, I am just a shell,

Trapped in a silent, endless hell.

I long to sleep where I belong,

In your arms, where I was strong.

To rest my head upon your lap,

And whisper all the pain I've trapped.

Do you know what it's like to breathe,

Yet feel like life has left beneath?

To ache so deep, to break so slow,

Yet wear a smile so none will know?

I could cry an ocean wide,

Or let the silence be my guide.

Hoping one day, you'll truly see—

The love, the loss, the missing me.

Love, sleep has turned its back on me,

My mind a prisoner, never free.

You live in every restless thought,

A war I fight, yet never fought.

Please come back—it's getting tough,

The nights are cold, the days too rough.

I know you'll come, I hold that fate,

But love, I beg you—don't be late.

Each day I call, though there's no sound,

Just to see if walls break down.

If maybe, just for one soft breath,

You'd set me free from love and death.

It hurts, but I still stand tall,

Loving you despite it all.

So take your time, but hear my plea—

Don't be too late to come to me.

I knew you'd leave—my soul had told,

A whisper soft, a warning cold.

Yet still, I prayed to skies above,

"Please, not this time—let me keep this love."

But fate is cruel, it shut the door,

Left me drowning, lost once more.

You walked away, no last embrace,

Just silence filling up your place.

Now my heart turns into dust,

Ashes born from shattered trust.

I try to breathe, but air feels gone,

I can't accept that you've moved on.

I still remember how sweet you were,

A heart so soft, a love so pure.

A fragile soul, too much to bear,

Scarred by wounds no one could repair.

And then you found me—I held you tight,

Taught you to laugh, brought back your light.

Stayed every second, fought the fight,

Against the world, against the night.

I gave you all, my heart, my breath,

A love so deep, I had nothing left.

I watched you bloom, I stood with pride,

Never knowing you'd leave my side.

You grew so strong, so wise, so free,

That even I became a memory.

And now I stand in endless rain,

Your love my joy, your loss my pain.

But still, it's fine—if hurt must be,

Then only you can do that to me.

So take my heart, take all of me,

For even now, I love you free.

Each morning, as dawn paints the sky,

My first thought is you—soft, lingering, nigh.

Perhaps you've forgotten, or maybe you care,

Yet silence has taken the love we once shared.

I never imagined a day would arrive,

Where your voice fades, yet echoes survive.

No touch, no whispers, no warmth to embrace,

Just memories haunting, time can't erase.

You left, yet you stay, a shadow unseen,

A love once vibrant, now trapped in between.

It numbs my mind, it wears me thin,

Yet through the pain, I love you still.

The day you left, my heart turned cold,

Or maybe I perished—perhaps I'm untold.

Maybe I breathe, maybe I survive,

But my heart? It no longer feels alive.

You never asked, never touched the wound,

A silent sorrow, forever marooned.

A pain that lingers, never to fade,

A love once bright, now lost in shade.

Now pills keep me here, prayers hold me tight,

Yet love for you grows, defying the night.

Against all odds, despite all pain,

My heart still calls—you remain.

I still remember your magical eyes,

Where I once saw my world rise.

They shined like the moon so bright,

Holding me close in their silver light.

When you looked at me, I always knew,

Your eyes whispered, I'm enough for you.

Not just me, but all could see,

The love that burned so endlessly.

But now, my love, they've turned so cold,

A distant story, left untold.

I search for warmth, for traces of light,

Yet all I find is endless night.

Has love faded, slipped away?

Or am I lost in yesterday?

I saw the pictures—frozen in time,
Your laughter brighter than even mine.
My birthday was never just my own,
It was your joy, your love, your throne.

I still hear the song you softly sang,
The way your voice through my soul rang.
Eyes locked, a love so true,
A moment eternal—yet gone too soon.

The gifts remain, untouched, untied,
But what I longed for was you by my side.
I never needed a day to claim,
Yet you made it shine in love's own name.

But now, my love, the light has died,
No wishes left, no stars to guide.
No birthdays now, just endless night,
A silent heart, a faded light.

No more candles, no more cheer,

Only shadows whisper here.

And when the day returns once more,

It won't be mine—it's yours to mourn.

My everything is tied to you,

In moments small, in shades subdued.

The clothes I wear, the air I breathe,

All still whisper that you once lived with me.

You are gone, yet never far,

Your touch still lingers where memories are.

The mirror holds reflections old,

Of love once warm, now lost and cold.

The empty chair, the midnight rain,

The silent echoes call your name.

I move through days, but not the same,

For everything still speaks your name.

The day we parted, the world stood still,

Your words cut deeper than time ever will.

You said we had no future to see,

Yet once, you swore you'd fight for me.

I stood there crying, lost, betrayed,

Wondering how love could so quickly fade.

Was this the same soul who held me tight,

Who promised forever in the darkest night?

You once defied the world for us,

Made me believe, made me trust.

But when the storm came, you set me free—

How easy it was for you, but not for me.

I cried, I begged, then anger came,

A shield to hide my endless pain.

Through trembling lips, I let it go,

Said "It's okay," but it wasn't so.

The words escaped, cold and dry,

Yet inside, my heart let out a cry.

For the moment I said I'd be fine,

Was the moment I knew you weren't mine.

A second passed, but it felt too long,

Like love had died where it once belonged.

You walked away, so easy, so free—

But that second still lives inside of me.

I stayed awake the whole night through,

Lost in the silence, aching for you.

Believe me, love, no night felt so long,

An endless darkness where you were gone.

The clock moved, but time stood still,

Every breath heavy, against my will.

The stars burned bright, but none could see,

The void your absence left in me.

No dawn, no light, just echoes deep,

A love once ours, now mine to keep.

And in that night, so vast, so wide,

I knew a part of me had died.

The next day, I reached for you,

Called again, but no reply came through.

Each ring echoed, empty and cold,

A silence louder than words ever told.

I sat there wondering, lost in pain,

Is this the same soul who once remained?

The one who cried when we missed a day,

Now turns away, with nothing to say.

How does love fade in just one night?

How do hearts change, lose their light?

I called, I begged, I held on tight—

But you had already let go that night.

I begged you, just once, to meet,

To look into your eyes, to find my peace.

I thought if we sat, if we spoke,

We'd mend the love that never broke.

But you refused, turned away,

Left me drowning in words unsaid.

I believed one moment could heal the pain,

But all I found was endless rain.

My chest ached, the weight too strong,

My friends saw what was so wrong.

They pleaded too, for one last sight,

But you were already lost to the night.

Tell me, love, was it that easy?

To walk away, to leave me pleading?

While I gasped for air, for just one sign,

You let me fade, as if never mine.

You gave me your reason, and though it tore me apart,

I swallowed my pain, hid my broken heart.

I understood, despite the ache,

Yet all I asked was a farewell to take.

But you refused, afraid to see,

The tears that once mattered to thee.

You said you'd break, you wouldn't survive,

Yet, my love, I was barely alive.

You feared regret, but not my pain,

Left me drowning in endless rain.

You couldn't stand before my eyes,

But could bear my silent cries?

How could you watch me fade so deep,

Where even breath felt hard to keep?

If leaving was love, if distance was kind,

Then why did it leave me half-alive?

I begged the world to reach for you,

To whisper my pain, to pull you through.

And after endless pleas and cries,

You agreed—but placed time in lines.

You came, but love felt caged,

A meeting bound, a heart enraged.

And it hurts, oh love, to recall those days,

When time with you would slip away.

We once sat for hours, yet never enough,

Now minutes felt like too much to love.

How did forever shrink so small?

How did you build this unbreakable wall?

You once held me, endless and free,

Now you counted seconds to leave me be.

And love, if time was all we lost,

Why did it feel like I paid the cost?

You came, I saw you, but love had died,

The warmth was gone, the spark denied.

You weren't the one I once adored,

Not the soul my heart swore for.

You stood before me, yet felt so far,

Not my sweet, soft morning star.

The innocence, the love, the light—

All had faded into night.

And in your eyes, I saw the truth,

A silent farewell, cold and cruel.

You weren't here to hold me tight,

You came to leave, to end the fight.

That day, my love, I lost it all,

Not just you—but who you were before.

For the girl I loved was left behind,

And all that remained was goodbye in your eyes.

You said the world wouldn't let us be,

That love must bow to destiny.

I saw the weight upon your chest,

The silent war, the quiet unrest.

I asked of you, just once, to fight,

To stand with me, to hold on tight.

Not against the world, not against fate,

Just trust in us—before too late.

I saw the pressure in your eyes,

A love trapped beneath the lies.

Yet when I begged for one last stand,

You let go of my waiting hand.

I would've fought, I would've bled,

But you chose silence instead.

And now I stand where we once grew,

Fighting alone—for the love we knew.

For you, everything mattered—everything but me,

And love stood last, too blind to see.

Do you know how deep it burned?

How every silence left me spurned?

From the day you walked away,

Tears never let my heart betray.

When I met you, eyes turned red,

A storm of sorrow, words unsaid.

I searched your gaze for what was lost,

For reasons why love paid the cost.

But you mistook my shattered eyes,

For anger sharp, for cold goodbyes.

How could you think I'd wish you pain,

When all I wished was us again?

If love was there, strong and true,

How could you not see what I still do?

I asked you, how can it be so easy?

How could love fade so completely?

And then you spoke—the words so cold,

"I've been detaching… letting go."

But love, what about me?

Was I meant to break so suddenly?

While you slowly erased me piece by piece,

I was still holding on, begging for peace.

Your decision fell like a crashing wave,

Swift and ruthless, no love to save.

While you had time to drift away,

I was left to shatter in a day.

You had months to loosen your hold,

I had seconds to watch love grow cold.

And in that moment, lost and small,

I realized—I had lost it all.

I still remember that beautiful day,

When you called from the airport, on your way.

I rushed to you, heart so light,

Eager to hold what felt so right.

By fate, we wore the same hue,

As if the universe already knew.

You laid your head upon my chest,

Held me tight, found your rest.

But love, I didn't know—

That moment was your final show.

The last time your heart was mine,

While I dreamed of forever, you counted time.

You knew, yet you held me near,

Let me believe, kept me dear.

And love, the cruelest part of all—

You left before I could fall.

Before I could show how deep I feel,

Before I could love you beyond what's real.

You walked away with all we were,

And left me grasping at empty air.

When you said, "Time is over, I must leave,"

I begged like a child, too broken to breathe.

"Just two more minutes," I whispered low,

"Let me love you before you go."

But love, you didn't soften, you didn't stay,

You raised your voice, pushed me away.

For the first time, I saw you cold,

A stranger in the love we used to hold.

And in that moment, through tear-stained eyes,

I chose your peace over my cries.

So I let you go, though it tore me apart,

Held my love, but silenced my heart.

For if staying meant your sorrow grew,

Then leaving was the last love I gave to you.

I stood there, helpless, watching you leave,

Surrendered to your happiness, though I couldn't breathe.

Seeing you for the last time, love,

Felt like a knife, yet I couldn't rise above.

Each step you took, it cut me deep,

But still, I prayed your peace to keep.

Even as my heart bled dry,

I only wished it wouldn't reach your sky.

You'll never know the pain I hide,

Of watching my everything step outside.

Of standing there, numb and cold,

As love slipped through the hands I hold.

And after you left, I couldn't move,

Like life had lost its only groove.

My soul—you—walked away that day,

And all that remained was an empty me in your place.

I still remember the day so bright,

When "I love you" danced in your eyes like light.

A thousand times, you whispered true,

And in your words, my world grew.

But love, then came the darkest night,

When you swore upon me—no love in sight.

Your voice was cold, your gaze turned gray,

And in that moment, you walked away.

It didn't just break me—it burned me whole,

Turned my heart into lifeless coal.

From endless love to empty space,

You left me drowning in your erased embrace.

And now I stand, lost and torn,

Between the love we had and the love now gone.

From thousands to none—it's all so strange,

How easy it was for you to change.

The second you left, I faded away,

Like I never mattered, like love was a stray.

You erased me as if I was never real,

While I stood drowning in all I feel.

You looked at me, but not as before,

Not with warmth, not with love—nevermore.

You mistook my eyes for something cruel,

As if my love was meant to wound.

But love, these eyes never wished you pain,

They only prayed for you, again and again.

Even in heartbreak, they searched for you,

Hoping you'd see what still was true.

Yet, in the end, you turned away,

Hating the love that chose to stay.

I loved you more, and that's my crime—

To hold on when you left me behind.

And you know, love, what's the worst of all?

I let you go—I had no choice at all.

Not because I wanted, not because I could,

But because your happiness was all I understood.

I wanted to hold on, to fight, to stay,

But love is cruel in its own way.

So I chose your smile over my pain,

And in doing so, I broke in vain.

I thought letting go would set you free,

But in the end, it only caged me.

For while you moved on, untouched, unknown,

I was left to fight the dark alone.

Loving you meant losing me,

And now I'm lost in what we used to be.

After you left, I fell into the dark,

A night without stars, a life without spark.

Endless shadows, no way through,

Yet my heart still reached for you.

But love, you built a wall so high,

Stronger than tears, colder than goodbye.

Not even my blood, not even my pain,

Could touch your heart or call your name.

I screamed, I bled, I tried to fight,

But you had shut me out of sight.

And now I stand where love once grew,

On the other side, still missing you.

I let you go, love—I set you free,

But even then, I kept reaching silently.

Not to hold you back, not to make you stay,

Just for one last talk, to take the pain away.

You spoke your side, you said your part,

Then walked away, leaving my broken heart.

But love, what about the storm in me?

The words unsaid, the agony?

I thought you'd calm the fire inside,

That before leaving, you'd stand by my side.

Just one peaceful moment, just one last trace,

Of the love we built, of your warm embrace.

But instead, you left me there to fall,

Shattered pieces against your wall.

You left in peace, without a fight,

And I was left to battle the night.

You thought I was overdoing, love,

But you never saw what lay beneath.

I was the one who never knelt,

Who lived with dignity, strength, and belief.

Yet for you, I shattered my pride,

Begged with hands once firm and tied.

In front of all, I fell so low,

Just for a talk before you go.

Not to keep you, not to fight,

Just to end this pain in light.

But love, you turned away so cold,

Leaving me lost in stories untold.

I lost myself while saving you,

And still, you never even knew.

I was the one who never knew fear,

Lonely, yet strong, year after year.

Darkness was my quiet friend,

A world where I could stand, defend.

But love, the day you walked away,

Everything in me began to decay.

The loneliness I once embraced,

Now haunts me in your empty place.

The darkness I never used to mind,

Now whispers echoes of you behind.

You were my light, my guiding flame,

And without you, love, I'm not the same.

After you left, love, I fell apart,

A lifeless body, a broken heart.

I was so close to slipping away,

Yet all I wanted was for you to stay.

Not to hold you back, not to plead,

Just your voice—that's all I'd need.

A word, a touch, a moment near,

To ease the ache, to calm the fear.

But you closed every door, every way,

Left me drowning, pushed me away.

And love, the pain you gave to me,

Was beyond what a heart should see.

Beyond human limits, beyond control,

Yet even in ruin, you were my soul.

My loved ones begged, their tears fell free,

They cried for me, but you didn't see.

Not once did you turn around,

Not once did you hear the sound—

Of a love that once was pure and true,

Now left dying, calling for you.

And I stood there, lost in thought,

Is this the same love I once sought?

The girl who once held me near,

Who wiped away my every tear?

You grew up, love—you changed so fast,

Turned your back, left me in the past.

The one who once feared my smallest pain,

Now walks away as I call in vain.

You were my sweet, innocent light,

But now you stand, cold in the night.

You've grown so much, love, it's true—

So much that my death means nothing to you.

I remember the day I was slipping away,

Weak, broken, with nothing to say.

Hospital walls waited cold and white,

Yet all I longed for was your light.

My loved ones begged, their voices shook,

Asking you to just take a look.

One word, one moment, one trace of care,

But love, you weren't even there.

"It's none of my matter," you said so plain,

Like I was a stranger, like love was in vain.

And in that moment, more than the pain,

Your words carved wounds that still remain.

For you, love, even the strongest fell,

A heart once fearless, now a shattered shell.

I stood unshaken, against the tide,

But without you, I crumbled inside.

I tried to fight, I tried to stand,

But the weight of loss was too grand.

Love, I was a fortress, steady and tall,

Yet for you, I lost it all.

And in the darkest hour of my endless fight,

I thought of ending this cruel night.

Not for escape, not for release,

But just to find a moment of peace.

Sleep became a stranger to me,

As memories echoed endlessly.

Everything I touched, everything I knew,

Was tied to one name—it was you.

Even the air carried your trace,

A silent whisper, an empty space.

The nights stretched long, the days felt cold,

Fear replaced the love I used to hold.

I wasn't afraid of the dark before,

But now, love, I fear even more.

Not the shadows, not the night—

But a life without your light.

And you know, love, I tried it all,

Tried to rise, tried to stand tall.

Like you, I tried to hate your name,

To burn the love, to end the flame.

But love, no matter how hard I tried,

Hatred never grew inside.

Because the truth, as cruel as fate—

We cannot hate the ones we love,

Even when they teach us pain.

I looked at your pictures, at the ones of us,

Every smile, every touch, every promise of trust.

You once told me, with love so true,

That forever, you'd create memories with me and
you.

But love, if memories bring only pain,

If they echo loss, if they drive me insane,

Then I would rather have loved you not,

Than be left with a love time forgot.

For what good are moments that tear me apart,

That weigh like stones on a broken heart?

If love was meant to bring such ache,

Then maybe, love, it was my mistake.

You know what hurts me the most, love?

Not just that you left, but who you became.

The girl I held, the one so kind,

Now stands before me, cold and blind.

I once knew you—soft, innocent, true,

A heart so pure, a soul that grew.

But now you're stone, unshaken, untamed,

Even when I'm drowning in endless pain.

Even a stone would have melted, love,

Seeing me break, seeing me fall.

But not you—you turned away,

Like I was nothing, like love was small.

And so a doubt lingers in my mind,

A whisper that haunts, cruel and unkind—

Did you ever love me at all?

My heart and mind became a battlefield,

A war for you that never healed.

One screamed, "Move on, let go, be free,"

The other whispered, "But love was she."

My heart still held you, soft and true,

Refusing to believe I lost you too.

But my mind, tired and torn apart,

Tried to bury you deep in the dark.

Yet no victor rose, no peace was found,

Just endless echoes, a hollow sound.

An inner war with no resolve,

For love like ours can't dissolve.

I stood dry-eyed at every goodbye,

Even as loved ones closed their eyes.

I never wept, never broke,

Held my pain in silent cloak.

But for you, love, the dam was torn,

A flood of sorrow, deep and worn.

I cried like my heart would tear apart,

Like the ocean was born from my heart.

Tears that no loss had ever seen,

Tears that drowned the man I'd been.

For love, I wept as never before—

For you, love, and nothing more.

You know what's worse, love?

The pain I carried, the weight I bore,

It wasn't just mine to suffer alone—

Even my mother saw it at its core.

She saw the hollow in my chest,

The silent wars, the sleepless rest.

And one day, I broke, I let it flow,

Cried in her arms, let my sorrow show.

"I love her, Ma," I wept like a child,

"My heart is shattered, my soul exiled."

And through my tears, I whispered slow,

"You don't know what I saw in her eyes, though."

For in your eyes, love, I once saw light,

A home, a forever, burning bright.

But now, even my mother sees,

That love has turned to memories.

Even my mother saw my pain,

Felt my heart break again and again.

She couldn't watch me fade away,

So she begged you, love—just to stay.

She asked for nothing, just a call,

A single word, anything at all.

But you stayed silent, cold, apart,

While I lay there, torn in heart.

And in the end, love, like always,

It was me who had to find the way.

With trembling hands, a voice so weak,

I called you myself, just to speak.

Tell me, love, was it so hard,

To ease the wounds, to heal the scars?

Or had you already gone so far,

That even my pain couldn't reach your heart?

They tried to heal me, to make me whole,

But none could reach my broken soul.

Their words were kind, their hands held tight,

Yet all I longed for was your voice in the night.

No medicine, no time, no plea,

Could mend the wreck you left in me.

If loving you meant losing breath,

Then love, I'd choose you—even in death.

Every day was a war I had to fight,

A struggle for breath in endless night.

I woke to pain, I slept in ache,

Survival itself felt like a mistake.

I lost each day, I lost myself,

A ghost staring from the mirror shelf.

The reflection hurt, the scars ran deep,

A man unrecognizable, drowning in grief.

And for what? For a love so true,

For a girl who once swore, "I'll stand with you."

Yet when the storm raged, when I was torn,

She never turned back, she never mourned.

You leaving didn't just break my heart,

It broke the man I used to be.

I lost my confidence, my fire, my soul,

I lost the very essence of me.

I stood before the mirror, empty and weak,

Eyes that once shone, now hollow and bleak.

Tears fell as I searched for a trace,

Of the person I was before this place.

And in the silence, a question remained,

Echoing deep, driving me insane—

"Do I deserve this endless pain?"

It hasn't been long since you walked away,

Yet my mind drowns in questions each day.

A storm of thoughts, a million "whys,"

Echoing loud beneath silent skies.

Did you ever love me, or was it a lie?

Was I not enough, no matter how I tried?

Did you forget me the moment you turned?

Or do memories of us still make your heart burn?

But love, I know—I'll never hear,

The answers my heart holds dear.

For you left, and with your goodbye,

You took my closure, my last reply.

The pain you left wasn't just deep,

It made me wish for endless sleep.

Breathing feels like a cruel test,

For life without you is nothing but rest.

If love meant suffering this way,

I'd have chosen death over this decay.

I still remember our final call,

My voice trembling, my heart in thrall.

I begged you, love, just to speak,

But you stayed silent, cold, and bleak.

"Is it that easy?" I asked through pain,

Hoping you'd say you felt the same.

But in a voice so sharp, so cruel,

You said, "Yes, it is"—as if I was a fool.

I told you, love, with a breaking voice,

"I have no one, not even me—only you."

But you listened, silent and cold,

And still chose to let me lose you too.

And then you spoke—

Not like my sweet, innocent love,

But like a stranger, distant and cold.

For the first time, I saw you change.

You spoke to me like I was nothing,

Like love had never been between us.

You asked me to leave, said you were tired,

Told me not to bring my pain to you.

That day, something in me died.

I became numb, silenced, lost.

The only thing I ever swallowed—

Was the disrespect from the one I loved most.

Even after all the pain you gave,

My love for you refused to fade.

I should have let go, I should have healed,

But my heart chose to stay, refused to yield.

And so, I hated not you, but me,

For having a heart that wouldn't break free.

A heart that loved despite the pain,

A heart that lost, but loved in vain.

And now, as the storm inside me calms,

My body trembles, too weak to stand.

The pain you left—too deep to heal,

Yet I bear it, though I can't feel.

I've accepted it all, the wounds, the scars,

The love that faded, the distance, the stars.

I've accepted your hurt, my shattered fate,

I've accepted the loss—as mine to take.

But you know, love, what hurts the most?

It's not just you, not just the ghost

Of all we were, all we dreamed—

It's the doubt your leaving has weaved.

Was it me, or was it fate?

Were the lines on my hands drawn to break?

For no matter how much love I gave,

Destiny still chose to take.

Whoever I held close, I lost,

No matter the love, no matter the cost.

One by one, they walked away,

Leaving me alone in the night to stay.

And now, after all that's gone,

I find myself where I've always been—

In the same dark room, all alone,

Haunted by what could have been.

This time, I collapsed in that room,

No light, no hope, only gloom.

Every door is locked, every path erased,

Lost in a silence I cannot escape.

The walls whisper the names I've lost,

Echoes of love that came at a cost.

And here I lie, with no way through,

A prisoner of memories, trapped with you.

There is no going back from here,

No hands to hold, no voice to hear.

The past is gone, the doors have closed,

And I must walk this path alone.

I have to live with what remains,

The silent nights, the endless pain.

No escape, no second chance,

Just a life without your glance.

And now, I have accepted the truth—

I never existed for you.

Maybe you never loved me at all,

Or maybe it was love that learned to fall.

But my love is not like yours, my dear,

It does not fade, it knows no fear.

Even when the soul is lost in cries,

My love remains—long after it dies.

My love, I have realized this—

I don't need you to love you.

I can love you in silence, in absence,

Beyond touch, beyond sight, beyond time.

I can love you till my last breath fades,

And even beyond death's embrace.

For true love asks for nothing in return,

It simply burns—forever, unshaken, unturned.

I loved you like the moon loves the tides,

Pulling, longing, yet never collides.

A silent force, unseen, unfelt,

Yet shaping worlds where love once dwelt.

I am the candle, burning bright,

You are the wind that stole my light.

Yet even when my flame turns blue,

Its warmth still whispers only you.

A river flows though never kissed,

By shores it longs but must resist.

So too, my love, I let you be,

Yet carry you like waves to sea.

For love is not a hand to hold,

Nor just a story left untold.

It is the echo in the night,

The fire that lives beyond its light.

In loving you, I lost myself,

A book unwritten, left on the shelf.

I will never be the same again,

A soul once whole, now drowned in pain.

The day you left, you took my heart,

Carried it far, tore it apart.

And with each step, with each goodbye,

You stabbed it more, yet left it alive.

Now love feels like an empty name,

A hollow fire without a flame.

For how can I love, when love is you?

And you are gone—like the morning dew.

If my sorrow gives you peace,

If my suffering sets you free,

Then let my heart remain in pain,

Let my nights be lost in rain.

If my brokenness soothes your soul,

If my silence makes you whole,

Then I will bear this endless strife,

And live like this my entire life.

For love was never mine to keep,

But to endure, to burn, to weep.

And if my ruin brings you ease,

Then I will shatter—if it means your peace.

Remember this, my love so true,

I loved you once, I still do.

And long after time fades away,

My love will stand, it will not sway.

For you alone, through joy or pain,

Through burning sun or endless rain,

If ever a tear falls from your eyes,

I'll be there—no need for cries.

Not as a shadow, not as a ghost,

But as the love that held you close.

Unseen, unheard, yet always near,

A promise kept—forever clear.

Don't be sad, my love, not ever,

I wish you joy that lasts forever.

May love and laughter light your way,

May happiness in your heart stay.

And though you walk a path unknown,

Remember—you are not alone.

You have me, my shoulder strong,

Even if you've been gone too long.

Never think of turning back,

But if you do, no love you'll lack.

I will wait till my last breath fades,

Even if you never return my way.

Forgive me, love, for letting go,

For burying the pain I'll always know.

Not by choice, but by fate's cruel hand,

I must walk alone on shifting sand.

There are burdens I must bear,

Dreams to chase, wounds to repair.

For my survival, I must forget,

Yet every step feels like regret.

To erase you feels a crime so deep,

Like stealing stars from skies that weep.

But love, if I must fade from you,

Know my heart still beats for two.

My love, this is my final call,

A whisper carved upon my soul.

Know that I will always stay,

Even as life pulls me away.

Your eyes still hold the world I knew,

A beauty timeless, pure, and true.

Don't regret the pain you gave,

For it's the last gift I'll always save.

A thousand loves could never be,

As dear as the wounds you left in me.

But above all, I chose your peace,

So I set you free, though I'm in pieces.

Be happy, love, that's all I ask,

Let joy embrace you, let it last.

And if you ever feel alone,

Know my heart is still your home.

You are no longer mine, I know,

Like a river that's lost its flow.

Yet in my heart, through endless time,

I remain yours—forever mine.

Seasons change, the stars may fall,

Yet my love outlives them all.

I ask for nothing, not even a sign,

Just remember—I'll always be thine.

My love, if not in life, then in death,

Let your shadow fall upon me once.

If my breath must fade unseen,

Let your eyes be the last I witness.

I do not ask for love reborn,

Nor a promise carved in stone.

Just one last glance before I go,

So my soul won't leave alone.

Come before the silence takes me,

Before my heartbeat slows to rest.

Let me hear your voice once more,

So I may carry its echo to my final breath.

Promise me, love, you will come,

When my voice has forever gone numb.

Stand beside the silent stone,

Let me not be all alone.

Whisper my name to the midnight air,

Let me feel that you still care.

Say "I love you" just once more,

Like a wave returning to the shore.

No flowers, no tears, just you and me,

In that moment, wild and free.

Even in death, I will wait,

For love like ours defies all fate.

Promise me, love, when I'm gone,

You'll stand where the roses mourn.

Whisper my name to the silent sky,

Let the wind carry your last goodbye.

When earth takes me in its embrace,

Let your voice be my resting grace.

Say "I love you" one last time,

Even if it's only to the grave that's mine.

No tears, no sorrow, just one vow—

That you'll be there, then and now.

For even in death, I'll wait for you,

In every star, in every dew.

And My Love, I love you most.

85

A Message to My Readers

Through every word, every tear, and every heartbeat
I've poured into these pages, I hope you feel what it
means to truly love—beyond time, beyond pain,
beyond even the boundaries of life itself. Love is not
about possession; it's about presence, even in
absence. It's about giving, even when nothing is
returned.

Never regret loving someone, no matter how much it
hurt. Love is not a weakness; it is a gift, a rare and
beautiful fire that not everyone has the strength to
carry. If you have loved deeply, you have lived deeply.
And that is something to cherish, not mourn.

Even if love is unfulfilled, even if it fades from
another's heart, let it remain in yours, for love is never
truly lost. It transforms, it teaches, and it stays within
you as a reminder that your heart had the courage to
feel, to give, and to embrace the most profound part
of being human.

So love fearlessly. Love selflessly. And never let the
world make you regret